Favorite Books

Mrs. King said to her class,

"I am going to get some new books

to put in your reading boxes.

Tell me what your favorite kinds of

books are,

and we will make a graph.

Then I can get the books

that you like best."

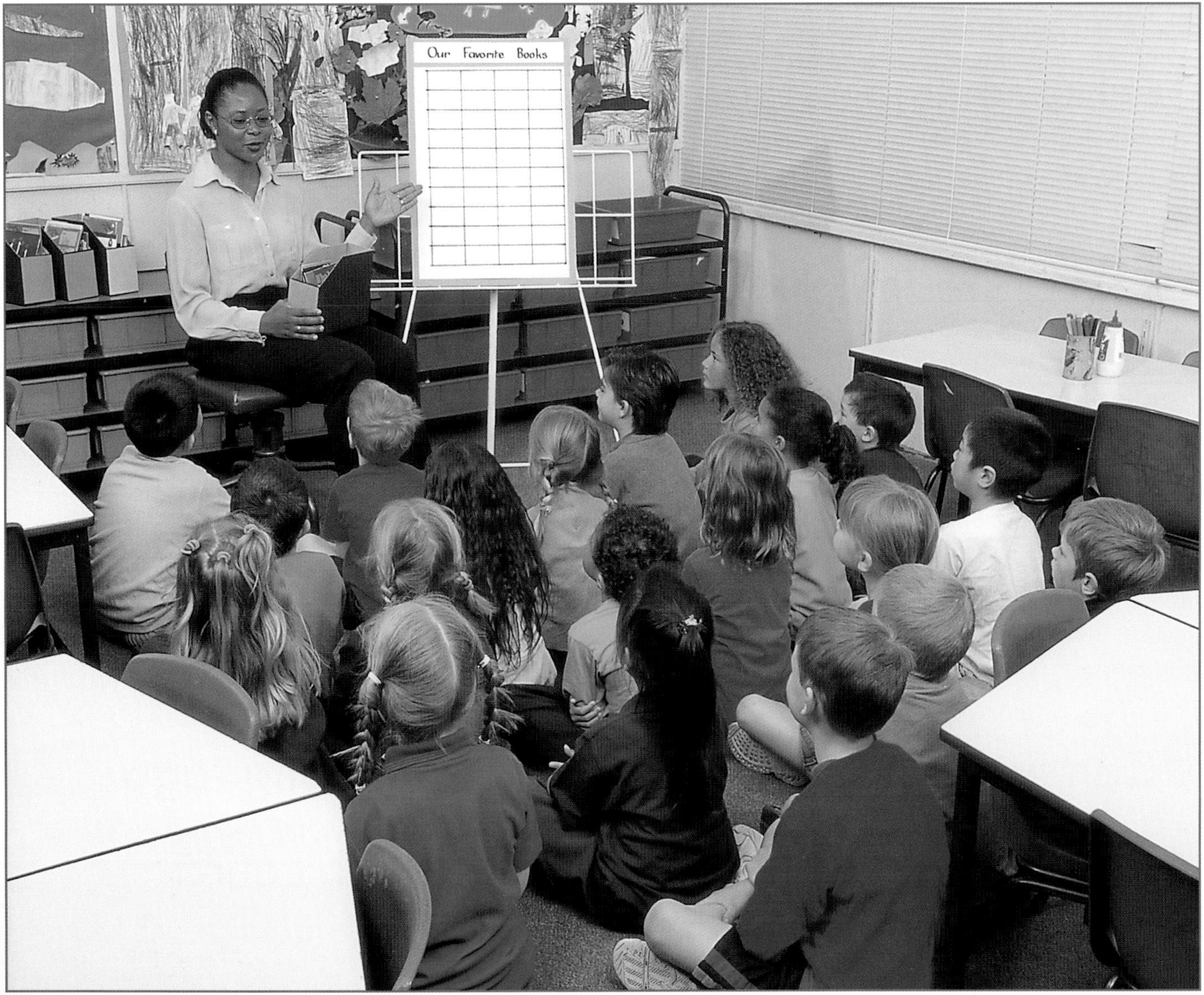
Our Favorite Books

"I like animal stories," said Thomas.

"I like stories that make me laugh," said Jake.

"Can we have some books that show us how to make things?" asked Nathan.

"Can we have some stories from long ago like <u>The Three Little Pigs</u>?" asked Laura.

"Let's make our graph first,"
said Mrs. King.
"All of you can put your name
on little cards.
Then we will put the cards
onto the graph.
It will show us what books
you want me to get."

"My card goes here," said Thomas.

"And my card goes here,"
said Jake.

All the children put their cards
onto the graph.

"The graph shows us that five children
like animal stories best,"
said Thomas.

"Then I will find five animal books,"
said Mrs. King.

"And we want six stories
that will make us laugh," said Jake.

"Four children like books
that show them how to make things,"
said Nathan.

"And five children like stories
from long ago," said Laura.

"I will look for all the books
you want," said Mrs. King.

13

Mrs. King put twenty new books
in the children's reading boxes.

"Making a graph was a good way
for us to get the books
that we like to read best,"
said Thomas.

Our Favorite Books

	Animal	Funny	Making	Long ago
10				
9				
8				
7				
6				
5		Jared		
4	Pesche	Nadia		Katie
3	Isabella	Jake	Oscar	James
2	Thomas	Chloe	Pera	LAURA
1	India	Athena	Nathan	Taylor
0	Simon	JOHN	Noreen.	Tilly

Five **Animal** Stories

Six **Funny** Stories

Four books for **Making** Things

Five stories from **Long Ago**

16